# SEQUOIAN

# SATORI

## Poetry

## &

## Wisdom

Devin

Masterson

# IMAGINATION EARTH

*IMAGINE*

*DESIGN*

*CREATE*

## *Acknowledgements*

This book was made possible by generous support from my friends, teachers, and loved ones. Thank you to the folks who see and accept me. Jennifer Erik, & Jeremy Masterson, Sophie Layman and her parents, Bruce Owens, Matthew Souzis of the Whybrary, Magi from Bolinas, Blake Foster & Jules Olmos, Merlin & Becka Miller, Josh Hutch's Gems & Minerals, Ashwin, Andy, Josie Bear, Natasha, Sebastian Dobron, Joseph Stelnicki, David Feris, Claudio Labra, Jessica Jane, Trevor Mahaffey, Elena & Elli + Windtree, my friends at the Esalen Institute, Marsha Hudson & Norman Brown from the Love & Power Institute, and the Sequoia Sempervirens Coast Redwoods outside my office window.

### What is Sequoian Satori?

Shortly before publishing, I began to research Coast Redwood trees and the etymology of their Latin name, *Sequoia Sempervirens*. These majestic beings are the tallest and most massive tree species on Planet Earth. They inspire me to constantly reach for the light, while staying grounded in the Earth. *Sempervirens* is Latin for evergreen or in other words, forever flourishing. I found this meaning to be a motto and mantra for life. Green as in a beginner's mind yet always growing quietly. Throughout the journey of this book, I've grown by tiny tea sips of *satori*, the Japanese word meaning to suddenly know, understand, perceive, or become aware one's true nature, enlightenment from ignorance. I seek satori through writing creatively and by simply walking through the living poetry of the forest. Thus, I named the book to mirror my practice. However, I uncovered a fascinating mystery behind the word *Sequoia*.

To be honest, I am certainly not enlightened or academically qualified to write about linguistics. Although I am indeed a curious poet that is dedicated to language and the fresh hot truth, so here we go!

Sequoyah (1770-1843) was a great Cherokee scholar who invented the Cherokee syllabary and alphabet around 1821 after studying languages for most of his life. A rare achievement by a single human, perhaps the only instance in our known history. Sequoyah is revered as a heroic visionary by the Cherokee people because he gave them the gift of literacy in their native tongue, allowing the preservation of their culture when their way of life was endangered. Learning this alphabet was so intuitive for native speakers that Cherokees achieved a 90% literacy rate by 1830, while only 70% American settlers could read and write at the time. Today our global literacy rate stands at around 87% as linguists continue to study the Cherokee language and alphabet as an extraordinary miracle of human communication.

However, some miracles are surrounded by immense suffering. Just 10 years after the invention of the Cherokee syllabary by Sequoyah, an atrocity occurred in 1831. The U.S. Government and American settlers committed a crime against humanity by forcing the Cherokee people off their ancestorial land in the southeastern states to Oklahoma in a death march known as the Trail of Tears. Unfortunately, we are seeing similar events in America, the Middle East, in Africa, and our very own hearts in 2025. I poetically protest and speak out about these acts of cruelty in this here book. Sequoyah and his people's very existence was threatened just as they experienced a renaissance of literacy and story. I can only scratch the surface of this legend, so I will provide a point of relation before offering you to dive deeper. While recovering from the Trail of Tears, the Cherokee Nation sent funds to the people of Ireland in 1847 during the Potato Famine as an act of solidarity against colonial oppression.

Thus, whenever I sit under a Coast Redwood, I now think of Sequoyah, the Cherokee people, and my own Irish ancestors with a reverence for humanitarian and Earthly solidarity against oppression.

As I researched, I hoped that the name origin of Sequoia Sempervirens for Coast Redwoods, was indeed Sequoyah himself, however there is much more to the story. Before I continue to another surprising truth, I must promote cultural education rather than misappropriation. When we become aware and empathic with good intentions, we build bridges for reciprocity instead of extraction or dominance. We can honor Sequoyah's contribution to the preservation of Cherokee culture by encouraging others to understand his life, the Cherokee's story, and their language. If you are fortunate enough to know members of the tribe, please be mindful and sensitive with your curiosity.

Please also consider learning about and supporting First Nation's reconciliation efforts currently underway around the world. Tread lightly folks and remember that we are guests of Mother Earth on shared land that has been stolen throughout history.

So, what is the etymology and origin of the Latinized word Sequoia according to the academics? This question has been the topic of debate and myth for decades without a definitive answer. I found a publication by Dr. Nancy E. Muleady-Mecham from 2017 that I've sourced for this section. Dr. Muleady-Mecham is an adjunct professor at Northern Arizona University and Columbia College with a PhD in biology and was a Park Ranger for 30 years. She has studied Giant Sequoias as a scientist rather than a feral poet like myself, although I do wear glasses and know a PhD or 2. According to her paper, an Austrian librarian and botanist named Stephen Endlicher

(1804-1849) created the genus name *Sequoia* in 1847, just 4 years after the passing of Sequoyah. Dr. Muleady-Mecham traveled to Vienna to conduct primary research by reading Endlicher's journals, publications, letters, and local even newspapers. Endlicher was a linguist, librarian, theologian, and botanist who became a taxonomist known for identifying plants and naming species new to the western world. He was well known by linguist circles, science journals, and the Western plant nerds around the globe.

Endlicher suggested the name change from *Taxodium Sempervirens* to *Sequoia Sempervirens* because he discovered unique characteristics of the species while comparing field samples. He was sent a sample of the Coast Redwood by an explorer to help further the pursuit of the scientific method. Keep in mind that Charles Darwin hadn't published the *On The Origin of Species* until 1859, so evolution was an unknown theory at the time. Interestingly, Endlicher had never traveled to the Americas or witnessed a Redwood Forest in person, but he was a renowned botanist, academic, and was known to study indigenous cultures. He was certainly knowledgeable about Sequoyah's alphabet and legacy due to his interest Native American studies. Dr. Muleady-Mecham confirmed a local newspaper's mention of Sequoyah and a colleague of Endlicher's writing on the same achievement of the Cherokee syllabary. But did Endlicher choose the word to honor Sequoyah or was it because he was a scientist using Latin?

Endlicher was known for naming plants after people as was common practice in science at the time, but he was also fascinated by plant medicine, math, language and culture. For example, he named the feather flower from Australia, *Verticordia huegelii* after Carl von Huegl, the Austrian explorer and botanist, famous for his tour of Asia and Australia. Dr. Nancy E. Muleady-Mecham's research also found that Endlicher collaborated with fellow scientists intimately familiar with Sequoyah's syllabary and he was likely impressed by the man's achievement. She concluded that Stephen Endlicher probably latinized Sequoyah into Sequoia due to his respect for an extraordinary achievement by a fellow linguist and a pattern of naming species after luminaries.

However, that's not all folks. Another academic named Gary Lowe had sought to debunk this 'myth' in 2012 by advocating for a more mathematical and Latin taxonomy explanation. He followed up with another book on the same topic in 2018. We are at a crossroads of myth and science, but maybe the answer is mixture of both realms?

Lowe explains that Endlicher arranged the conifer genus taxonomy by the median number of seeds per cone scale. You can still identify a conifer species by simply taking a sample of the number of seeds per cone scale. The triangular fish scale looking growths that makes up the spiraled structure of the cone each contain a few seeds. Endlicher was a numerologist and a linguist, thus created his own sequence of 1,3,4,6,7 to explain the difference in median number of seeds per cone scale for each species of evergreen conifer. Redwoods or Sequoias have a median of 6 seeds per cone scale on average, according to Endlicher. Thus Gary Lowe argued that perhaps Endlicher used *sequor* - to follow in Latin, to refer to the math sequence found within the genus. Even if Lowe is incorrect, this is an astute discovery by Endlicher. In Lowe's 2018 book, *Debunking the Sequoia Honoring Sequoyah Myth*, he explains that this story began around 1856 with a quote: "The honor must be intentional; but if not, the accident is most gratifying." However, there are no known sources from Endlicher himself to determine the truth because he passed away just 2 years after the naming of the tree.

In my own hermeneutics, I interpret the truth to be all inclusive: the story of Sequoyah, Endlicher's Sequence, Latin, plus a divine mystery. Endlicher knew the story of Sequoyah's syllabery and understood Latin like a priest of plants. But was his choice a wink from Spirit to remember the Cherokee and the Earth? I'll let you decide after consulting a Redwood tree on a foggy mid-morning.

What will you learn after sitting with the tree and your thoughts? My friends that is called: *Sequoian Satori.*

**Muleady-Mecham, Nancy E.** "Endlicher and Sequoia: Determination of the Etymological Origin of the Taxon *Sequoia.*" *Bulletin of the Southern California Academy of Sciences*, vol. 116, no. 2, 1 August 2017, pp. 137-146.

**Lowe, Gary D.** *Debunking the Sequoia Honoring Sequoyah Myth: The Naming of the Original Genus of the Coast Redwood and Giant Sequoia.* Livermore, California: Lowebros Publishing, 2018.

# Contents

# *Introducing...*
# *Sequoian Satori*

   Well, this is a grand experiment which may succeed if at least one of you describes this book with accidental beatnik poetry in public. I hope this imperfect act, yet honest tree pulp manifesto thing inspires some fellow rebels and renegades to get after it and be the change that our world so desperately needs. I hope that someone deletes ChatGPT, loses their phone for a week, and solves big problems with their friends over a meal. I hope that we start walking alone and hitchhiking to work until we trust each other again. I hope that someone reads this and runs to a library to learn about Sequoyah and then spends a day under a Redwood tree with nothing but a scroll and quill until they know their vision. I hope that we may walk in beauty together as one to remember who we are, why we are here, and where we came from.

   I'd be remiss not to mention that Mother Earth and Spirit have graciously bestowed upon me a few gifts: my mentors, kind family, the wilderness, and lovely friends who walk me home to my heart, where the great mystery of poetry resides. My teachers Matthew Souzis and Bruce Owens have helped me to find my voice, patiently teaching me to surrender. My friends listened to what that voice had to write and shared their own truths. I am forever grateful to these humans, including you the reader. While poetry is an act many of us commit in secret, few of us will admit to our reverie. If the spirit moves you to celebrate language, our fellow beings, and the Earth, then please carry on brave one!

<3 Dev

# Step

# By

# Step

Hold my hand and walk with me,
pockets full of faith and responsibility.

As we step into the labyrinth
of loving possibility.

# Table of Questions

The questions below can be used as 52 weekly queries for a ponder and a wander or as chaos magic poetry prompts. A friend realized that this ponderosity also creates an oracle deck by using a standard deck of cards with each card assigned to one of the 52 questions. I'll let you decide how the numbers correspond to the card suits for an oracle that is uniquely yours. Remember that asking ourselves questions and finding answers is only the beginning of self-understanding, it's the journey of discovering wisdom that reveals our truth.

1. What's true for you now?
2. Who are you?
3. Why are you here?
4. Where did you come from?
5. Who do you love?
6. Who loves you?
7. Love, what does it mean to you?
8. How do you 'walk' on Earth?
9. Why do you walk and where?
10. Who relies on you?
11. How are you important?
12. Why do you care about our home planet?
13. What's going on around here?
14. What does your soul need today?
15. Why did our planet get so messy?
16. Who's gonna clean this place up?
17. How can we work together?
18. Who needs a hand?
19. How can we consume less and give more?
20. What am I willing to give up so that others can have more?
21. If you listened to your senses, how do they feel and why?
22. What does gratitude look like for you?
23. What emotions are longing for you to feel and express?
24. How can you become an interdependent member of our community?
25. Where do you find peace?
26. What does home mean to you?
27. How can we listen to each other?
28. What can I learn about life from our solar system's celestial bodies?
29. Do you really need that thing on amazon?

30. How can we reduce waste?
31. What can we make with what we've got?
32. Do trees love music and why?
33. What's your dream and how could you try it today?
34. Do hummingbirds dream of flowers?
35. What would a wooly mammoth and a whale say to us?
36. Why do some animals alter their consciousness just like us?
37. How much food can you find for free in a day?
38. What plants near me are edible?
39. What if food didn't come in plastic?
40. Who would I want to walk home for their last time?
41. If oil didn't exist, what would the world be like?
42. What can we learn from just being?
43. What can plants teach us?
44. What if the same shit that's in the ocean, land, and air is also in our bodies? Are we one being?
45. How might you emote more honestly?
46. Where does our waste go and why?
47. Compost much?
48. How could you make amends with the person you've hurt the most?
49. What has Mother Earth been waiting for you to say?
50. If you could tell anyone they are forgiven, who would it be? And why?
51. What does this planet need that you have?
52. If you could change anything, what would it be?

# *Alone*

Letting go into what is here with you.
No fear, forgetting the phone.
I'll find the way home, on my own.
All I need
is sunlight to see the sky,
my heart shall guide the way
to the dreams that never die.


6/1/25 | Soquel, CA

Written to Peace Sine's bass waves on a beanbag
under Sequoias at a Soquel, CA property beyond 4
creek crossings traversed via a grandpa's Prius.

# An Athenian Day-Dream at Midnight

*(for Zeus, DaVon, and Faeryn)*


Pomegranate bergamot elixir meets cacao chai
serum,
and the mythologian meets Mount Olympus himself.
Magenta light beams
tickle dusty subwoofers
in the Blue Lagoon at early spring.
There's a thickness in the air,
a heavy steam of arousal,
and allure peeking around corners.
Freedom dances in all dimensions and
expressions.
Toppings of rose hips and coconut filaments on
cookies
for sweaty hip swayers
to power on through
to ecstatic self-emergence.
Relationships tended, forged, and magnified
by the grace and glory of our community.
Bass rhythms rumble cheeks
into enthusiastic whirlpools and eddies
flowing along a melody creek stream.
A spectacle of Saturnalia to behold,
an experiment of
an Athenian day-dream at midnight.
The clock stops
as these playful creatures find their muses
at teatime for a little dress up magic.
It's a Dionysian inspiration
for us to reawaken
our most aliveness of human beingness!

March 29th, 2025 | Santa Cruz, CA


Integrated after a Greek mythology inspired soiree
at an infamously rowdy and sloshy dive bar.
Juxtaposition of visionary magic and stale craft
beer becoming malt vinegar under jukeboxes.

## Attachment

Our favorite pen gone away,
full notebooks forgotten, damn WiFi is broken,
hours of a day. Oy vey.
Like a rose dropping petals,
the way we worry away perfection,
as today catches air in hours.
Allowing our lotus to open,
attachments fall away like expired flowers,
revealing a new day's freedom alive in the dawn.


July 31st, 2024 | Meditation Cushion

## *Autumn in Sonoma*

Golden brown and reddish yellow
grape vines line the hills
as the harvest moon rises to say hello.
Friendly black phoebes
and hungry sparrows
flutter among
drying oak canopies.
Families gather
to savor the season
of gratitude
and squash aging attitudes.
Cinnamon and nutmeg
spice the eggnog
with flavors
of jovial hand holding
and easy goin' rhythms at play.
Before we pour our wine,
let us tip our hats
to the Miwok people
who stewarded the land
on which we're standing.
Ancestors shining blessings
with the wise eyes
of them twinkling stars.
Now let this season
remind us
of the reason
we've come so far.


11/24/23 | Sebastopol, CA

# *Balthvs**

What if
music and community was more than the sound?

One can only wonder at night
under that starlight and silence,

because the notes are a moment,
but now is forever.

And when we dance to 3 souls playing as one,
we ARE more than the sound
 way more
   way Way out there beyond the doors

and here at the same time.

9/25/25 | The Catalyst in Santa Cruz, CA

*typed to the beat of BALTHVS on a 1971 Remington
Sperry Rand Streamliner at the back of the
Catalyst theater.

BALTHVS (BALL+Thus)

## Beatae Memoriae

(of Blessed memory and my first poem as a poet)


Summon your burden
Recall a ponderosity
Conjure some compassion

Relent, unload, tenderness.

Empathize the unforgotten
Float on through heaviness.

Exhale exasperation
Inhale inspiration
Unpack and re-create.

Unbundle the burden
Unwind, untangle, untie.

And gaze upon a fellow kind eye.


3/25/23 | San Francisco, CA

# Be Cool Now

Dip off the 1 to the left, off the pavement to where gravel crunches under firestone tires as ponyless carriages ferry by. Brrrt over the dots. Between traffic, you can hear the slow rush and pull of the ocean lapping at the cliffs. Sipping on sandstone, misting teal into fog, green ice plants spill off the cliffs into the dunes. Artemisia sage brush layers onto the dewy afternoon with a twist of hemlock to remind you of the velvet rope separating poison from medicine. Homeopathic psychics know the wilderness of difference. Against the young cliffs is a bonfire burning oak and emanating smiles to the twilight. Around the flame is a circle of stones, watched by the eyes of friends, patiently awaiting your arrival.

Like Ram Dass, but hip to the 2025 milieu, they say:

"You're here! Be cool now"


2025 | Davenport, CA

# *Bells*

(For our lost ones and those they leave behind)


When the bells of grief coming ringing,
let the sound of a blue wind
sing for the heart's longing.
Listen for teardrops tapping stone
and remember that love is creative,
even fearless alone.
Recall their smile
that touches your soul
and let it soothe your suffering awhile.
Sit with the time
when you could smell their scarf
or the scent of their breath in a hug.
Feel that place in you
that is one with them
and hold the blues,
nodding yes to mother please
like a newborn baby muse.
Cry and coo with them,
sing praise and wish grace,
laugh some, and thank God
for the all the fun
and good times
that make us one.


March 6th, 2025 | Santa Cruz, CA

# *Belonging*

Way up on Empire Grade,
far from today's dues
and yesterday's news unpaid.
Tonight is shire in dune,
sci-fi fairies flying in costume.
A promise of theatrical whimsy,
spiraling mystery,
and a little magical zipse.
Artists cast of stardust
skipped into ol' fern gully.
Kindred sillies
ready
to play
their hearts
fully to the trees.

The kind of place where even a bully
might say sorry,
hallowed grounds so mutually holy.
We nodded a silent motion of hear ye, hear ye,
let this evening be safe
to feel free
ever so please.

Redwood fairy rings held us
like reunited siblings
hugging after years of longing.
Our bare toes and fair soles
nestling in duff,
soft and forgiving.
Oak, sage, and mama ganja smoke
wandered
between revelers and pure Sequoian reverie.
We played catch with laughs
and prayed with our hips to dance at last.
Mixing moments of ecstasy
with sweet surrender to happy destiny.
Becoming one with creation,
all elements present,
even the aether tasting of elation.
Ideas invited as guests for tea,

thinkers puzzling truths,
golden teacher mushroom mystery
soothing fellow seekers.

The spice of life
revealing the dharma of the cosmos,
a little cinnamon, pepper, and cardamom rose.
Freaks found wisdom tinkerers
of the ancient's lost hermeticism.

Time dilating
to a halt
before zipping past the future.
Each second
slipping
down
the pendulum strings.
Crashing sound waves
lapping
at the coastal seashells in our ears.
Mavens of joy rejoice,
morning ravens toy their voices
to eager beaver volunteers.

Benevolent sunshine opening eyes again,
towhees and warblers
singing
good day my dears.

The forest listened to our songs,
the redwood roots warmed by our moves,
and Mrs. Mother Earth smiled upon her children.
She said...

You belong right here my loves.

You
Belong
Right
Here
My
Loves

June 2nd, 2024 | Bonny Doon, CA

# *Beltaine*

Midway between the equinox and solstice,
it's a day when sunshine sky hawks exalt us.
Medium in meadow play,
sweetness of labor justice,
and a celebration
of our Earth's own goodness.
Let the fairies swirl, the dervishes twirl,
the swallows swoop, and the kiddos whoop.
It's Beltaine in May,
springtime air unleashed
upon green grass dancing
together in peace.


May 1st, 2024 | Bunny Meadow, Golden Gate Park

# *Be. The. Overview. Effect.*

Our extra perceptual friends
are post physique and without pretense.
They live in the infinite
and commune
through the static
of electronics and curious spirits.
We can divinate their teachings
via entheogens, dreams
and light beams.

They're preaching

the sacred chorus

of universal oneness.

And they've found the keys to consciousness,
sharing their clues
with playful ease.

All they ask

is that
we love one another,
sing together,

and preserve
our Earth Mother.


11/28/23 | San Francisco, CA

# *Beyond*

Look out around you for the magic.
That speck of dust or floating feather in a gust,
it's all right here and now,
just waiting
to be seen and plucked.
Zoom in for the fungi
and way out for the eagle eye.

There's a whole cosmos of happenings
Beyond

just You and I.


12/24/25 | Earth, Milky Way Galaxy

# *Big Sur*

The grand southern coast, where the ocean crashes
into crumbling cliffs and dark skies. When the
forest meets the tides. From friendly library
attendants to sulking bar maids, the folks here
march to an upside down beat unlike any other.
Dramatic sunsets and theatrical locals make a
motley scene fit for a mystery novel or perhaps a
mythical fable. The scents of artemisia
sagebrush, fennel, and cypress pair perfectly
with a spliff and a splashing IPA. One day there
may be an open road, or this feral island will
become a fairy tale commune. Ungovernable,
impassable, yet radically charming and serene.
Just the way life in Big Sur is meant to be.

12/14/24 | Big Sur, CA

# *808 Bippin'*

Lonely cars on empty streets
with a clear view
that's just
a smash away
from silica dust.
You remembered to lock your doors
but let go of your toys you must!
A friendly neighbor peers through,
he says it's just window shopping…
Except you're the one who's buying.
The glimmer of a silver necklace
that alluring ketchup packet,
the corner of a dollar no less.
Spark plugs and CRASH, the car window goes SMASH!
Like a cat in a bird's nest,
a banker in the till box,
a man under the dress.
The alley pirate tosses the console,
he pillages with a drum roll,
And unbuckles his misdemeanor.
Alas, it's just some broken glass,
a bit of cash,
and them streets gettin' a little meaner.


2/28/24 | San Francisco, CA

## Blacktop Disco Chic

The iridescent asphalt glistens
as streetlights cast faint shadows.
Brick buildings numbered and initialed
to signify their dignity with specificity.
A glowing fortress of L.E.D. canteens
beside a line of revelers
begging for a bumbling synchronicity.
A crowd dressed after dark in blacktop disco chic
and buzzing as they are ushered
into the rumble
of nighttime bliss.
The air smells
like the port of Oakland
with wisps of honey bucket,
but it sounds like a party
you don't want to miss.
A man in a white jumpsuit
alerts ground control
to begin the launch sequence
before we depart.
Earthlings check their boots
and find their seats
on the robot heart shuttle
to fly into the frequency
of sonic art in orbit.
Ambient rhythms
begin to sing
as a guitarist plays jazzy blues
like a physicist solving ancient algorithms.
Deep bass drones
through the steel and concrete
to invite the first astronaut
to space walk in their Levi's denim.
Co-pilots join the controls
with psychonauts entranced
by novel improvisations.
We're invited
to consider the sensation
of seeing Earth from space
to remember exactly why
we've been loved since birth.

I wrote this poetic account to integrate a cinematic ambient music performance by Eduardo Castillo at the Loom in Oakland, CA. He surprised us by bringing with him a jazz guitarist that he met the day before at the Guitar Center music store. Local legend Rob Garza from the band Thievery Corporation joined mid-set to improvise live on the keyboard. The venue was intimate, seated, and equipped with a custom sound system tuned to the large room.

This project was created as a homage to the Overview Effect, which is phenomenon experienced by astronauts who first witness the Earth from space and psychically know a reverence for our planet. It's an interconnectedness of humanity, self-transcendence, and a totally life-changing moment. The first person to feel this moment of Satori was Soviet pilot Yuri Gagarin in 1961. 10 years later, American astronaut Edgar Mitchell had such a profound experience on Apollo 14 in 1971 that he founded the Institute of Noetic Sciences (IONS) to research consciousness and parapsychol-ogy. Noetic is derived from the ancient Greek word *noein*, meaning to perceive, and associated with the intellect in modern times. IONS had their Earth Rise center in an Oak Forest south of my hometown Petaluma, CA. The Earth Rise center later became the Hoffman Process retreat center where I leaned into my healing journey in 2022. Noetic Sciences man, far out!

11/29/23

# *Boomtown*

Who is San Francisco?
A gold rush legend?
A techie at wits end?
A burner's last disco?
Greyhound bustop shake down or earthquakes on
steep streets long ago.
This city is an alchemical compost heap,
a venture capital vulture,
phoenix asleep in the fog.


It's not New York, because it's queer and quaint.
From its humming red bridge and tarot tower to a
rainbow light show for sweet Harvey Milk's love.
Counterculture seeps into the sidewalk graffiti
on Howard How Weird miracles.
Hippie hill drum circles on 420,
flea market tent town on fenty.
Mission immigrant magic,
and marina trust fund cappuccino karen mayhem.
We had an Alcatraz occupation,
an almost Americano Human Be-In revolution.
North Beach Vesuvio
began a beat poet lingo revival,
high on red wine justice, reefer and jazz.

Buy a ride on Golden Gate Park buffalo meadow
to see where them freaks go to flower.
We punk right wingers that whine fiasco
with a middle finger and some psychedelic heroes.

So San Francisco's magic will always prevail,
she's too wild to tame,
too radical to go lame,
and she will always be the same.


2024 | Mission District of San Francisco, CA

# *Bush on a Bluff*

The lone rose bush perched on the ocean bluff,
it's buds sipping mist, roots trading in duff,
solar power spiraling DNA…
all this to bloom
just a few floral fornication
honeybee hover stations.

Perhaps that scent of rose
is evidence
that nature rests in light,
meeting miracles time.

And that fleeting flowers
are just
sublime guests for teatime tonight.

July 31st, 2024 | Big Sur, CA

# *Business Thyme*

In a manic world of busy bees
and fast coffees, I sip my tea.
As the cyclist sprints
and the hummingbird zips,
the hot rod rumbles,
and the barista trips,
I breathe…
between
my impatient fits.
Just like a flower
that waits
to savor the sun
and seduce the bees,
I wave for fun
and spruce up my steez.
I'm hardly late
to bathe
in a free day
as I sip my tea
on a winter matinee.

2/22/24 | Coffee Shop Somewhere, CA

# *Calling*

Hold my hand and walk with me.
Can't you see that standing tree?
He breathes our laughs
and sheds his leaves of past.
Can't you hear that finch's song?
How about we dance along?
Why not toss our shoes into the brook,
our toes lost in the sweetness of dew and moss.
Have a look at the golden grass,
what a treat to see the wind wave and toss,
like your hair flows,
not a pause between the to's and fro's.
Smell the sage on the bee's wings,
feel the mist of the morning,
and sense our great belonging,
as we sing to beyond,
our spirit's calling.

2024 | Petaluma, CA

# *Canopy*

Along a winding path
of green clovers
and yellow wood sorrel,
what sorrows thou hath?
A drop of blues,
a dollop of melancholy,
A quip at tomorrow's news.
Let the air carry falling leaves
and the wind slip the swallow's muse.
Two butterflies
flutter in the morning sighs,
a dove sees the one as it coos.
Fresh eucalyptus mist
and sunshine peeking
through hushed lips.
A bird's nest wiggles
between creaking bends
of wooden bush tips.
The first chirp
of a baby bird
sends sonic love beams
to capture our sweetest dreams.

2/14/24 | Santa Cruz, CA

# *Cathedral*

A sauntering arrival as a guest in the Redwood
Bay Laurel cathedral, these elders listen for you
to pronounce your presence with:

"Awe, Wow, and thank you for having me over again
and again my friends."

A fern whispers for you to run your hand among
their green fans like the wind.

Sunlight is leaking through the trees, iridescent
in spider web streams, rays alive from the
heavens to your eyes. Say *ko-morebi* in Japanese,
to speak of Zen with the eloquence of a full
breath in oil of Hinoki Cypress from the East.

You hear the trickle of a cool creek swimming
down the curves of the forest basin, painting
flickers of light into periwinkle sounds.

Aging more slowly now to a total pause, an
intermission, to soak your soles in cold water,
the warblers sing above with an applause, sand
slipping by your toes as though an hourglass that
just turns and turns. The air smells of fertility
and renew, as ions drift into your snout to
purify that thought loop roundabout. You've been
losing sleep to cycles of what ifs, who did I
miss, and was that my phone buzz-ding-A-ling
again or just the jingle of my keyring against
the copper rivet in my denim pocket.

And yet the cathedral laughs on, for this slow
saunter is birthright medicine free for all who
meander among her and any who seek the wisdom of
the Redwood Bay Laurel elder.

5/16/25 | Henry Cowell State Park, CA

# Circus Freaks

On New Year's Eve 2024, my girlfriend and our friends went to see an adult's only circus in a Macy's parking lot in Capitola, CA. While the performance was intended for mature audiences, there was a nostalgic wonder about that the whole shebang, reminiscent of a dream or when magic's secrets were still a mystery. It was wholesomely adult content in an artistic way, rather than crude. This was acrobatic theater with a small dose of vulgarity and non-nude sensuality. The storyteller in me was studying how the performers masterfully energized the crowd building suspense and then releasing the tension as the crowd gasped, then laughed. This pattern repeated in waves that trended upward towards the climax of the show, almost like a trance music set or a sexual experience with freak power under the hood.

This delightful show was the regionally infamous Flynn Creek Circus. Their red tent with white stripes stood whimsically on asphalt beside a shopping mall. The pointed tent was a playfully defiant and sign-less beacon beside an American abomination of concrete decorated with lit up logos. What was the real circus freakshow? A hoard of middle-aged shopaholics high on credit cards and a Starbucks caramel-mocha-coconut Frappuccino or some vagabond badass acrobats and sexy clowns turning our worldview upside down? I guess that will always be Victoria's Secret. The juxtaposition of circus vs consumerism was perfectly played. Like the jester had set up camp right outside the King's emporium to juggle a royal collection of vases, while the court swine watched in horror as they clutched their pearls.

We arrived late, slightly tipsy, and the tent flaps were sealed shut with no greeters to be found. So we went around to the backstage area, following the sound, and slipped under a rope to end up in a corral of vintage airstream trailers. We were in the hum of generators and fumes that reminded us that time is money. As we were swiveling around to scheme our entrance, some smiling and spring-stepping performers caught us lurking. In their sequined strides with dramatic makeup, they motioned gracefully to follow them like they were expecting us. Perhaps my silver velvet tracksuit and my girlfriend's jingle bells, fur robe, and rainbow make up said: "We've got stage presence!" Their excitement and showbiz baby vibe had us thinking they were about to whisk us on stage for some improv clowning, but they sat us in prime seats with a wink.

We missed the whole introduction and background of the show, but we sat down at the beginning of a new act, perfect timing. A sparkly and sensual acrobat frolicked her way on stage, music drumming up suspense, the smell of popcorn in the air. She was joined by an older bald man with a hat in hand, their dance routine began like a courtship between two tropical birds. Slow stepping, eye contact, flapping wing gestures, side-stepping, artfully sensuous, body push and pull. As I watched the dance, I thought that circus arts seemed to either accelerate or delay aging based on how the performers treat their bodies, a universal truth of sorts.

These performers dazzled us with a flurry of flying arms and hat switching, momentarily playing archetypal characters with each hat. They bounced along to old timey circus music with a dialed in choreography. The hat tricks were miming outdated gender role antics, casually swapping dominance while confronting the crowd's good manners and civility. The symbolism of the act was a brilliant balance of collaborative clowning, choreographed antics, and a powerful deconstruction of masculine-feminine social constructs. The pair escalated the crowd energy with partner acrobatics, ending with the man on a unicycle with the woman standing on his shoulders as they swirled hats between each other to a grand applause. I had an aha moment, realizing that story telling like circus performances is all about building emotional suspense and then releasing the tension with a dose of humor, sensuality, chaos, or insight.

I won't spoil the rest of the show, but it got a little risqué with some sensual choreography and an older drunken couple gettin' frisky in their seats at the front. I love to see old folks being feral, 4 smuggled wine coolers deep with frazzled grey hair flying a freak flag, at the circus no less. I was poetically fascinated by the radical expression of pure human spirit, like getting lost at a Walmart in the South after Friday night lights.

While this was not my circus, I was surely one of the monkeys craning my neck in awe. I forgot to mention that our friend was one of the most daring performers, his long blonde dreadlocks whipping around with his wide-eyed airborne Tarzan stunts. My memory got fuzzy, but I will claim that he was launching himself across the stage on trampolines, trapeze, and springboards. Danger got the ladies going and the leggy acrobat babes got the guys riled up. After the show, we spilled out of the tent and Tarzan man joined us as our squad was engaged in wacky banter, amped up on circus freak power. The aroused old couple cutely stumbled into the backseat of a taxi, stinking of booze and pheromones. You go grandpa!

From the clowning and acrobatics to the paradigm shifting theatrics, we experienced a full range of emotions. Fear, Sadness, Joy, Surprise, Lust and Desire, Frustration, and Wonderous Hilarity. Flynn creek was truly a paradise for the freak in me. I've never laughed so wildly in such steamy circumstances in public. Thank you to the circus vagabonds and their magic!

# Collage

Beginning with a twinkle of the eye…
to the bit of an idea,
where matter meets mischief.

When the artist sees the loose threads on the
drapery of life, they snip the ends,
tuck the folds, and dim the lamp light
to flatter us in chicanery.

The artist hears the curves of a bell
and feels
the rawhide hoof of a drum.

They taste the salty waves
on strawberries grown in rows by the ocean.

They connect the zipper with the button
and the ripple in the puddle.

An artist becomes a wrinkle
in the fabric of creation
as they play dress up with light, color, and
magic.

Gifting an iota of spirit, a hair of a muse, and
a handful of boundless grit,
they are the mediator between the divine
and the default plane,
a misfit graffiti pilot.

From that twinkle of ideation
to messy media amalgamation,
it's like watching jiu jitsu grapplers square up
before wriggling a pretzel into final form.

The artist gazes at the salt crystals on baked
dough and wonders how the cuboids would feel
falling through their open hands. They remix
societal norms into genre bending jazz, like sous
chef's of cultural fusion, scientists of vantage
vistas.

Perhaps this gift of insight
allows the artist to dive into the mystery's void
as they swim in the current of curiosity.
Returning to stream delight
upon the most vexing of quandaries.
Making history so sexy and polite society squeem.
Thank the heavens for the artists,
that collage our dreams.

7/20/24
On a reading of Collage:

I met a dude with an English accent and a
coolness about him at a bar in Big Sur. We were
chatting about life and creativity, so I asked
him if he was an artist.

He said: "I work in theater actually and I'm here
looking for inspiration."
I replied with: "Cool man! I like to perform my
poetry. I guess that's like theater. Want to hear
one about being an artist?"
He said, "Yes, Please."

And so, I theatrically read COLLAGE to him. He
said he loved it and then we cheered to being
creative and off I went. Perhaps he was
overwhelmed by words, perhaps inspired, who
knows, who cares.
Later, my friend at the bar told me that the
English accent dude was a famous actor named
Andrew Garfield and I still didn't know who he
was.
I said: "I don't watch much TV or movies, but
that's cool!"
My friend said that he played Spiderman in the
most recent Marvel films and then I blushed.

☺

# Condor

I am the condor
that surfs breezes over the coast
and I am the otter
that swims through kelp in waves.
I want to stretch my hands into the Earth
while an orchestra plays.

And I am the violin that splits the air
as my fear of heights and deep waters
disappear
into the rhythms of my strings.
I want the salty kelp
in my miso soup
to become the vinyl of a song I used to know.

I can be all of it at once.
The condor's stunts
with the otter's grace,
as the orchestra plays my vinyl
in the blue ocean's grey mist and waves.


January 3rd, 2025 | Big Sur, CA

# Cove

Crash goes marine washing machine water,
tumbling hollow stones
as the sea recycles sand in retreat.

Alone in Granite, Jade, Agate, and bleached out
driftwood remains.

Mid-day sun, light rays, and rolling waves.
I am only here for now,
the water pulling me home.

Sodium salt tingling my olfactory bulb,
Eyes spotting pearlescent fragments
of spiraled seashells
between mussels and mollusks.

A friend patiently gazes into black rock,
kelp bobbing, while gulls are gawking,
mocking our peace of mind.
Help us they say, we're just like you,
lost
in the playful mist
of a mystery today.

This cove is a cosm of creation,
a nook of timeless wash,
a gift to share in the shortness
of a moment to pause.


August 3rd, 2024 | Big Sur, CA

## *Covering Uncommon Ground*

Ancient rhythms weaving melodies
from faraway lands,
swaying bodies
through the air
with playful flair.
Old and young, holding hands
feeling so nostalgic,
it's almost magic.
Silly laughter at broken glass
after a gaffe from shaking ass,
we're just grateful
to dance at last.

9/9/23 | Felton, CA

# *Coyote Humor*

The last light fades at dusk
as songbirds say goodnight with a busk.
A waxing sliver of the moon glows
with Polaris casting faint shadows.
Distant laughter echoes through the valley
saying welcome to coyote alley.
Their eyes catch the twilight
like beacons of mystical trickery.
Edging closer and closer,
watching us with curiosity tonight.
Testing our fear and humor,
sneaking by the boundary
of imaginary reality.
Begging to know why
we don't laugh at their cry.


2023 | Sebastopol, CA

# *Cupid*

That moment when you catch a smile
like a butterfly on the breeze
arriving to make your day.
A feather tickles the back of your neck
and a shamrock lover catches your eye.
It's cupid's arrow rushing by your aura,
tingling your sensuous,
soothing that stay back stranger.

The arrow left a teardrop of longing,
an angel's eye
in a mirror of light.
Within that drop is love, everything alive,
all at once,
totally ok
with whatever cupid sends your way.


2025 | Santa Cruz, CA

# Cypress

Wandering among ancient trees
that whisper secrets
through their twisted limbs and weaving roots.
The Cypress leans into the wind
to say welcome home and listen in.
"Listen for my call of patient wisdom,
hear my creaking limbs
as a Cypress signal, sighing yes,
absolute acceptance is within us.

Everything is ok, all is done.
We Cypress say:
We accept the wind's jury of wisdom,
so we don't worry when our day will come."


2024 | Big Sur, CA

# *Desires, Dreams, and Dares*

I dare to see my creative projects
open my heart to the world.
I dare to embody my whole truth
from my loving vision.
I dare to deeply belong to this world
as a steward of Earth and all souls.
I dare to speak from my heart,
a truth so pure and vast
that awakens all beings.
I dare to honor my vessel
as a channel for the highest good.
I dare to foster, cultivate, and nurture
my most cherished relationships.
I dare to live sustainably and mindfully
to conserve precious energy
as I direct surplus to causes
most important to our world.
I dare to let go of my past trespasses
with the forgiveness of Mother Earth,
Father Sky, and the divine child alive in me.
I dare to go serve thee
courageously flowing
into infinite equanimity.


2024 | Santa Cruz, CA

## *Dish Dreams*

The duck pond of dirty dishes dreams
has soap suds, sponges, and spatulas
splashing water
into pearlescent light beams
on blueberry bubbles.

Clank, crash, thunk, and ding goes the washer!
There's a certain serenity of flow
to duckpond mastery.
Some sense of purpose
unifying one's motion with the swirl
of dirty-dish-duty doers the world over.

And Opa!
Or as this dishwasha says, Viva La Bubblah!

February 15th, 2025 | Santa Cruz, CA

# *Drum*

At first, it was dark. . . nothingness.
An everlasting empty void without meaning, or
even mystery.

Until, slowly, slower, shhh…
and CRASH,
BANG,
a blast of infinite and pure light.

The miracle of creation,
from the collapse of silence.
The first spectrum of colors all in one moment.
Expanding in waves,
rising and falling past forever.

And then like the first strum of a tuned guitar
or the thump, thump, thump
of a freshly tanned drum,
the music of life had sung!

A cosmos of radical reverence for every being,
each speck and spark now animated
by the sacred chorus
of universal oneness.

As musical ripples
streaming between the eyes of God,
we're seen and heard, one by one,
little by little.

Just as the stars begin to brighten
on a new moon evening,
may we remember to sing through our grieving,
and swoon to our lovers
most sweetness
of
being.

11/7/24 | Esalen in Big Sur, CA (written after
Gregorian chanting in the baths)

# El Papachango

Que Onda man, we're on our way
to dance out somethin' spicy.
Big boombox on beachboy boogie,
Hawaiian shirts flyin' with spliff smoke floatin'.
Summertime pheromones
swimming in the subwoofers
like stray dogs
barking in the barrio on a full moon.
We got El Papachango at Moe's
with hot sauce moves
and that jaguar fire.

6/27/25 Moe's Alley in Santa Cruz, CA

# *Envelopes in Heirlooms*

Our greatest lessons are hidden within a red
envelope in an heirloom passed soul to soul, each
ancestor folding their secrets into love letters
written just for you.

The light that presents our heirloom that we so
resent, has been awaiting our return to receive
what we've forgotten.

So when that simmer of resentment turns to steam,
in the heat of a moment, our heart reveals that
antique covered in dust.

Grace becomes the key to unlock the chest, our
surrender to the light, opens an envelope in the
heirloom.

The first letter is addressed to you, but left
blank, so you may grieve all the blessings you've
missed.

The next letter is from you, awaiting your prayer
of thanks for what you've been given, a life on
Earth with a view of the heavens.

7/26/25 | Santa Cruz, CA

# *Equinox Revival*

As the Earth rounds the orbital corner from
winter to spring,
our creek beds and gullies awaken
into yellows and greens.
Celestial orange, white, and purple hues
dot the biosphere
like sticky notes of good luck affirmations
on the garden fence.
Happy pollen nodes and dandelion fairy ships
sail through the breezes
that wave along the grass of homely knolls.
Towhees, Robins, and song sparrows chirp
on the equinox morning
to signal that it's time for sonic bloom.
Wayward wild children of the mountain
share their joy
as seeds of wildflowers in spring.
Our bounty of yerba santa and nettle arrives
in the dim nooks of meadows
as medicine for colds and allergy sniffles.
This is the annual grand revival of planet Earth
each spring.
Sit and listen as the bellows of transformation
breathe life into the surrounding river glens
and mountain valleys.
It's a magnificent display of rejuvenation
to dance into
each and every spring day!

March 27th, 2025 | Santa Cruz, CA

## Fern Gully – I've been here before

Plucks of the fern frond in wet morning air, dreadlocks dropping hair into decaying duff, the fashion of Birkenstocks and patched denim. Guitar strings played to the plant's taste for *Feral Sequoian Rhythms*. Hippies hanging from tiny tree limbs over dancefloors, a disco ball lit just right, and a sense of cosmic possibility. Palo Santo smokescreens over mirrors. Tired smiles say I know you, but not yet. Maybe one day, we'll remember that we knew each other already, just from looking inside, eye to eye.

The spring trickles on and on, as life itself, purely flowing out of the mountain,

like a fountain of freedom to revel in.

Space animals were flown in by 4-wheel planetary rovers, with their zebra furs, glitter curls, and dusty polka dot teacups adrift.

Our Bare Feet in the Earth

Safe to Be Aware of Exactly What We're Worth - Everything and Now.

5/18/25 | Somewhere, CA

## Friday Morning

A morning pitter patter
the familiar neighborhood chatter
of finches playing in water.
Drip drop in the gutter
and the flip flop
of pancakes in butter.
Isn't rain ever your lover?

(a Friday somewhere, one day with the windows
open)

# *Friendship*

Friendship is a dreamboat that sails the seas
of how are you
and returns to harbor full of favors
each evening.
Flying by the easterly winds that bring good news
of poppies and wood sorrel bloom.
In these waves of today,
our fellow sailors smile onward with grace
after missing the buoy of whoopsies
and I'm sorries
to find an anchor of it's ok
and I love you my bay.
Within this schooner of happy company,
plays a loom
weaving stories to find the rhythm in harmony.
Slumbering skippers sway in hammocks,
as wizards sight the stars,
while the magician points the compass,
and cooks sing in the galley between our feasts.
Thankfully the painters wrap up cotton candy
sunsets in dry canvas
to share the glory we've witnessed.
And oh look there's a school of dolphins
riding the wake,
flowing the surf, and ee-ee-ee
echoing
hello how are you my darling?
Won't you be my friend?

3/23/25 | Santa Cruz, CA

# *Gallery*

A gallery of beautiful beings, surrounded by
colorful things, makes for a wonderful happening.
If creativity begins with a spark, then this is a
bonfire. From abstract creations to painted
imaginations, the light had found its lyre.

(For a gallery near you or the nook by your
favorite tree)


2024 | San Francisco, CA

# *Golden Redwood Dreamin'*

Ray of gold, ray of gold,
shining light,
lead me to my goals tonight.
We plead to see
what's whole and right.
Bring the Earth's truth my tree,
a vision bold and bright.
Like golden redwoods, we breathe clean air,
our roots weaving good and unseen fare,
living in water, decaying duff,
being everywhere,
Can you see how rare,
yet we have enough!
Our fires burning to cast a dare,
ready to ride into the rough,
see Mother Earth,
so cool she just waves her hair.

Our host in community
is the forest we grow,
the seeds we plant,
the humanity we sew
When our bellows sing
prayers of health
and cares for folks,
our fellow beings
grow old as oaks.
As our bare soles
rumble in soil,
she sees
our whole DNA uncoil.
She chuckles
when the stock goes tumble,
slowly she toils
until our pride grows humble.
Her cathedral held us,
her love compelled us,
and now she sends
her golden beams
through the faith
in our own spell dust dreams.        June 14, 2024

# *Garden*

(For my Great Aunt Barbie)

The garden calls for tender reflection,
to bask in the sun of life.
Gentle breezes pulling and pushing.

Flowers listening
to moments between restless weeds
and reflecting on the patience of buzzing bees.
Hummingbirds zipping amongst old and young,
carriers of geranium nectar quicksilver
and sugary sound barrier breakers.

The garden cultivates a vitality from stillness,
gifts answers to lost questions,
and offers sweetgrass braids to our tired senses.

August 1st, 2024 | Big Sur, CA

## Good Morning Sun

It was mid-spring with finches singing
and dew drops on empty benches.
The green grasses and wild oats
smelled sweet,
as goats in boots made paths
through the shoots so neat.
Sandy gravel crumbled, crunched, and crushed
under my beach cruiser tires,
with my voice hushed.
Just before the lighthouse,
an old fellow
sauntered along the meadow.
He too felt the serenity
of the morning light with finches singing.
Ahead of him was his grandson
smiling and waving without a phone in sight,
"Good Morning Sun, Hi, Howdy Do, Hello Everyone"

# *Guests of War*

Do you think Mother Earth cares who started it?
What about the free spirits whose last dance
we forget?
And the children whose tears we cry,
the mothers whose sons and daughters must die.
While congress whines:
"But the bone and bomb economy
of my donor's profitability
and the charred skeletons
in the closet
of the homeland missile factory."

They forgot that our ally shall be forgiveness,
for we must all
grieve this sickness.
No woman should fear
what her baby will witness.
No man should worry
if his son would do this.
As we're all children of Mother Earth,
thus we must coexist
with peace and justice.
We must be honest
as we clean up this mess.
We must hold hands
as we bless those we miss.
We must trust
that only the children
know what's best.

Perhaps we can learn
that we are all
just here
as guests.

4/29/24 | Santa Cruz, CA

## *Grand Father, Mr. Bruce*

Why thank you, we all belong here he says, me,
thee, and we.
Full of witty wisdom, strikes a gong with glee.

A little trickster playing cards with words,
Smiling a twinkle, eyes drip a drop of love.

Gives so much, yet ask so little,
Strong arm, a light hug, a peaceful poet.

Quick to play a game, fast to laugh,
slow to judge, compassion to another's past.

A fellow beloved by all, we're neighborly
brothers and sisters to this old mister.

Gratefully alive without a doubt,
like an otter in the ocean floating about,
diving to depths retrieving delight for those a
little uptight!


5/16/23 | West Cliff Drive Santa Cruz, CA

# *Home*

This hearth has faith in grace
and our doors are open
to guests who bear no gifts.
We welcome those who speak truth
and walk softly in beauty.
Just good humor and bare soles on lumber,
no need for elephant or donkey mumbo jumbo.
We're team Earth party artisans
in this old Edwardian.
Above us is love and what's below is behind us.
And within this home, may enter all kinds of us.


2/15/25 | Santa Cruz, CA

# *Humilitree*

Have you ever been humbled
after going out on a limb
for the fruit of humor?
Maybe you branched out from modesty
to test your grip on authenticity?
Does the rough bark leave splinters
or does it create calluses and embarrasses?
Are there saplings of integrity peeping through?
Perhaps that twig in your eye concealed
the pearl before you.
When the moonlight peaks at your sour apples and
bergamot trunk rot,
does it reflect off your pride?
Or does it bathe your whoopsies with humilities?
That moonlight will play tricks
until you grab a staff
and start growing your own canopy
like DaVinci with laughs.
Sway your pendulum to remember
how forests grow into lumber.
Look back and chuckle at the orchard
that dreamed you awake.
Admit your knots and let the ripe peaches drop.
Be humble, extra please,
partner with another in the blue collar breeze.
Ask for a hand to find your roots,
offer your gift of time,
and grow your truth into an wise ol' Humilitree.


2025 | Santa Cruz, CA

# I dream of one world that

**sings** to the trees and laughs with the buzzing bees before it disagrees.
I dream of one world that prays for peace and prepares to live with ease because it's not all about the me, me, me's.
I dream of one world that listens to ancestors to learn about our futures.
I dream of one world that plays music to unite all souls and dances to the beat of our celestial goals.
I dream of one world that swims in the ocean of love and breathes the pure atmosphere that our generation cleaned without a need for greed.
I dream of one world that sees the stars, hears the birds, and feels the seeds in the palm of our hand.
I dream of one world that lives in harmony with the sacred chorus of our universal oneness.


12/25/23 | Sebastopol, CA

## *FourTet in San Frandisco*

There was an alien invasion of peace and love.
Some intergalactic
star-crossed lovers from above,
with hearts of stardust and minds of gold.
At the pioneer helm was our trusty captain Kieran
beaming up the palace
of sacred cows in all colors.
There was nothing to fear,
but how we may find our fellow travelers
as time unraveled.
Bass drums captured our hips,
snares pierced the air,
lights dazzled our senses,
strobes stopped the clock
and fractured our phobias.
Perhaps this globe can in fact come together
to love one another at last.


10/28/23 | San Francisco, CA

## *Heavenly Tea*

Steeping in sulfur springs
as my beard smells of campfire smoke.
The stars twinkle on the horizon,
like a candle in a hillside cabin.

As my shadow and light melt
into this mineral claw tub tea,
I sink lower and lower
until my earlobes touch steam.
I hear the ocean lapping at my toes,
the pull of the moon on my the heart,
the tug of cool gravity on my holy truth.

Seven chakra ports open to the milky way above.
Each window
a liminal slip
into the zodiac signs that read:
"Yes, my love!"

My soul's mineral claw tub tea
now floats on the sea spray
to meet the heavens that beckon me.


9/7/24 | Big Sur, CA

# Hot Chocolate and a Candle

(For my paternal grandmother, Editt "Judy" Masterson neé Nielsen. She was born in Denmark and was a lover of chocolate, butterflies, and almond marzipan)

Kindness tastes like hot chocolate
grown by benevolent hands
and sung with a valiant heart.
When Grandma graciously bestows you
with that first warm mug and a big bear hug,
a candle of love is lit.
Each moment together, every sweet kiss,
and all the laughs shared…
They fan the flame until it grows strong
with fairness and grace.
You may lose sight of the hot chocolate fire,
but it's embers glow on
through the dancing shadows below.
Tears of fright, fears of the night,
and yet the candle will never go out.
Those trials of curiosity
only serve as kindling of growth
because Grandma took an oath
to tend to your golden candle of light.


2024 | Penngrove, CA

I read this to Daniel Pinchbeck and asked for feedback. He said: "It's very hallmark…"

# *Imagination Earth*

What if we can imagine our way into living in
harmony with nature's generosity,
so we may become the creativity guardians of love's
possibility?
When we see the oopsies of yesterday
as opportunities for play,
we can give our open hands
to the grace of a maker's yes for today.
That loose plastic widget
becomes the fidget key
to unlock our creative tiger's cage.
Your broken bookshelf is now the perfect mix of
matter
to make an altar
that honors the make-do messiness of beauty.
Our hello soda can of aluminum allows uh, um, uh,
um
to become a recycled alloy with magnesium
that can one day carry medicine to save the
kindergarten of tomorrow.
Wherever we look, there is matter awaiting our
imagination.
No need to dig, drill, or dive because mother earth
provides everything we need to survive.
She only asks that we imagine each other existing
in harmony
as one big blue green beautiful being
mixed in the media that is the perfect present
moment.
It's our universe of yes please to the cycle of
life,
as we collaborate to regenerate our future
through pure imagination in the apples of our eyes.

September 2025 | Santa Cruz, CA

# *Leave 'em Be*

A squishy first step
off the set path.
From early suns pep
to a quiet moon's laugh.
A welcome perfume
of petrichor's musk.
The seldom bloom
of fungus before dusk.
We're on the hunt
for moonlight fruit.
See that little runt,
we're close to the loot.
Mercy me,
there's golden plunder
under that silly old tree.
It's nature's splendor,
a tasty treat,
chanterelles in butter,
better than meat!
But should we pick 'em,
and lick 'em,
or just leave 'em be
for the next fellow to see?


3/29/24 | Santa Cruz, CA

# Lessons on Life from Cleaning Toilets

(For my friends in CABinS at Esalen)

1. Service is sometimes invisible
2. Praying and porcelain polishing both happen on the knees. Surrender!
3. Missed hairs and mirror streaks are learning opportunities
4. Teamwork builds a relationship, but solo work builds grit
5. Laundry is symbolic for rebirth
6. A clean room lets guests relax into their journey
7. The things we ruminate on when cleaning are the edges of our growth
8. Every group has a jokester and a contrarian, let them be.
9. Asking for help before it's needed builds humility
10. A good attitude is contagious and free
11. Ask oneself why and how, then act swiftly with courage
12. When given directions, always repeat to confirm
13. Flow from your center, move with purpose
14. If everyone takes responsibility and does their best, we all succeed
15. If you can solve a problem immediately, just do it
16. Be the solution, like water!

2024 | Big Sur, CA

## Let Us Be One

As we witness fear and hate
of our fellow beings,
these anti's and phobia's
are not known to be freeing.
As children, we learned to be giving and humble,
to care together,
and to stand up for what's earnest my brother.
When we face the wickedness,
let us be honest
to the divine's forgiveness.
As great apes
gifted with compassion and ethics,
it is our duty to study
this world's history and mystery.
To remember the past as we create the present.
Like minerals about to transform
into crystalline gems,
it takes immense pressure,
great heat and the rearranging of atoms.
We are but stardust
that can study this universe of trust.
This strange privilege must be respected
with reverence of our power
to surrender into love.
Courage becomes accepting what's true
and forgiving what's not.
We must see the beauty all around
this tiny blue dot of glorious splendor.
Now let us choose
to be fused
as one
with grateful surrender.

11/2/23 | Santa Cruz, CA

## *Let you in*

When there's something I'm holding onto,
it's my past clash,
or a verbal skirmish,
except I'm scolding you.
There's a damned river
of tears between us,
and only a storm
that can free us.
A chip in big bad me's
armor dam,
let's you in,
to see me in the mirror madame.
Each time
we breathe a little softer,
we're healing
the wounds of our ancestors.
Slowly,
the river's banks
flood
with love's healing waters,
to carry us home
where all is forgiven and understood.


4/7/24 | Petaluma, CA

### *Look into the sacred mirror*

What if. . . the other was me?

Which parts am I afraid to see?

Why not…
speak softly,
holding the heart,
dissolving differences,
transmuting fears, critiques, and old wounds.

Why then, why not?

Now imagine feeling lighter,
floating above the fighter,
healing from a mourning doves coo,
and lovingly
seeing
myself in you.

2023 | Uvita, Costa Rica

## *Lonesome*

I'm walking with no one to hold my hand.
under the LED streetlights
that don't twinkle like Paris.
I forget why I'm lost, I wish I knew.
The quiet early morning air is static
like my thoughts stuck between
a station of jazz and past fights.
A stray alley cat,
the curious courier of lonely nights
stops me to say hello friend.
Her purr comforts me as I confess my soul,
she says this can't be the end.
Unimpressed with my human mess,
she waves her tail goodbye.
I'm alone again
with just the stars as my companions.
They twinkle at my friendship demand,
remembering those who walked alone
with no one to hold their hand.

10/9/23 | San Francisco, CA

# *Love is*

We all believe in love, you and me.
I see you doing goodness without notice.
I see you asking for nothing, but to be witnessed,
understood, and seen.
Love is and love does. It's giving life a chance
for a change.
Love is an apology in action
and invisible forgiveness.
It's that feeling when hope returns
After a year of depression.
Love just is.


8/9/2025 | Santa Cruz, CA

# Love makes Peace without war.

When we remember how to make peace before war within our own hearts, we'll be ready to join the rest of the universe.

-DM

# Moon Walking

Humans walked on the moon, and it was on television, groovy man, but what about the Earth? MLK Jr and JFK were both offed in '68, then Nixon was inaugurated in 1969 while young men were being drafted to 'fight' in Vietnam. Yet peace loving hippies and pacifists said: "Uncle Sam? Never heard of him, but I ain't no Senator's son."

Woodstock happened in New York with 400,000 attendees. Mutual aid provided most of the services and Jimi Hendrix played his famous psychedelic rendition of the National Anthem.

The Stonewall Rebellion begins the public facing gay rights movement after police raided a queer club in New York City.

Trial of the "Chicago Eight" begins. Activists stood up for the civil rights that we enjoy today.

**Abroad…**

The Beatles release *Abbey Road,* John Lennon and Yoko Ono staged a "bed-in" for peace.

Monty Python's Flying Circus debuts on BBC.

In post-war Japan, University of Tokyo student protests struck a chord. Their 'prophet' was a poet and self-educated philosopher named Takaaki Yoshimoto. He challenged the status quo with intellectual individualism as a remedy to the mass indoctrination and nationalism from WW2.

Lyrics from "Aquarius/Let the Sunshine In" by The 5th Dimension, 1969

*Harmony and understanding*
*Sympathy and trust abounding*
*No more falsehoods or derisions*
*Golden living dreams of visions*
*Mystic crystal revelation*
*And the mind's true liberation, Aquarius*
*Aquarius*

# Mom

Oh mother, who would I be without you?
You call when I'm feeling blue.
How much I think of you,
I wish you only knew.
I tell all my friends about you,
just ask them, it's true!
You taught me how to see beauty and to smile
cutely.
If I got an ouchie or was feeling grouchy,
you were always there to help me,
and you'd never leave without me!
When school was too hard,
you were there with a flash card.
Every time I was hungry,
you asked what we needed in the pantry.
You taught me to bake Zucchini
and how to cook fettuccine.
I helped you plant the garden
and you never made me feel like a burden.
You taught me manners, morals,
and to never rest on my laurels.
When I did wrong,
you let me say sorry,
even though I was quite headstrong.
Your integrity and humility
let me see
it was not all about
the me, me, me.
Your generosity for another family
taught me
to look for need before greed.
You showed me how to raise a puppy
and that I wasn't always so funny.
You helped me to pause
when we needed space
and were patient
when we weren't on the same wavelength.
You never gave up on me even when I thought you
were lame.
As I get older, I've grown proud of your name
because I know
we're one in the same.        4/29/24

## Moop, there it is.

It's found on the ground,
A thing a ma jig,
A Who's a what's it.
Pick it up,
a toy or twig?
A lost key
or
a feathered bee.
Maybe it flys?
Let's try and see!


## My 1st Grade Teacher was Mrs. Kellog

I couldn't read until age six,
learned slow and was afraid to let go.
There was no garden in the classroom,
no dog to chase,
and too many strangers with rules.
First grade was a shock
at a school built over my old field
with steel, concrete, and fresh tanbark
over my Petaluma farmland foul.
I rode my bike through the halls before
the classrooms had windows.
My teacher was Mrs. Kellogg from the bay
and she was sweeter than cinnamon tooth crunch,
but I was different, she had a hunch,
she sent the rainbow room
so I could learn to read,
and boy did they plant quite the seed.

10/22/23 | Petaluma, CA

## *Our Very Own Vaudeville*

Within each of us is an ancient lineage bound by
quantum entanglements that seek to unravel
secrets through our personal mythology. Karmic
mysteries leaking clues to ancestral missteps as
we stumble upon doors ajar with the light of our
psychology tickling at the cat's tail. A peek
into our past or an insight of precognition that
our soul is not for sale. In the doorknob, are
the keys to the ignition. The metaphysical is not
superstition, but a polarizer on the lens of
reality that enhances our senses. As we realize
that we're each God playing chance until we learn
to dance to the beat of our very own vaudeville
in the chapel of light and shadow.

2024 | Santa Cruz, CA

## Owl

Looking out and into you.
Seeing what you've forgotten or left behind,
the tracks, the footsteps of the hare.
With a stroke of a white feather,
she says you hurt me there.
She flys away to leave you
hungry and alone, but aware.
Embarrassed, you missed the prints,
but remiss
that this life
is
a lonely bliss.


6/23/25 | Highway Vista at Midnight, CA

## *Peace Tricks*

Inside the divide of strange times,
there's a child with a wise vision
beyond the division
to unite the rulers with spicy rhymes.
Trickery and Tom foolery,
despite despots' derangements.
Confusing propagandists through clever insights
that defy power and diffuse idiotic infights.
Disarming the nukes
with Democratic clownery
that rebukes authority
ever so gently.
Peaceful statements of playful defiance
to find humor
in fictional boogie men alliances.
These enemies of joy,
cower at the laughter
from their own selfish blunders.
As dictators swear off their missiles
when the people watch fear
fizzle into clean air
with a prayer
and walk freely
through imaginary borders.
My dear,
wouldn't that be
just and fair?


2/5/24 | Santa Cruz, CA

# Quadruplify You Butterfly

Let open wings flutter and flap
Each section in tandem, no crap

Green and gold light, air just right
Thank you cocoon, please gratify these wounds,
we're flying soon

Another Friend floating by, proof, witness of
brave finesse

Must accept the gust, dew to mist, mottled glare
goes flare

Jolt of fate, glimpse of the beyond, time to fly

Ground control to major Tom

All Whole, whoosh whoosh,
let's prance for the prom

Aloft, self-sustained, instincts in action,
BLAST OFF

Creatures go guffaw,
that hungry grub woke up in awe

You outgrew the musing of yearning blues, small
talk behind

One small YEP to the plan,
one giant leap for all kind

Thats right, you earned it,
gO Onnn and dOooo the Locomotion

Fly up high,
you defy feeble notions of smallness
in sacred slow motion

Take a hokie pokie,
skank a spritely eccentric stride

Follow the flow,
speak beauty fellow,
bravo,
it's bonafide.


May 10th 2023 | San Francisco, CA

# Red Bandana, Ponytail Flying*

(I was up on Summit Road and met a man named Mark)

Happy pirate, Los Gatos mountain man Mark was a storytellin' about bird dogs and duck huntin'. One leg wobbles, but he don't need no cane, only sunshine and hardwork, some days just supervisin' with wit and charm. I was a weedwackin' and he goes, you better come back tomorrow, same spot, same time, they'll be bigger than when you started. He knew the weather for today based on how creaky his knees were a week ago.

He's the Cat daddy of a rabbit snatchin' and lizard snackin' 20 strong pride, you betcha they're intact, just like spirit made em'. A PBR can in a worn koozie and a lit Seneca dart in the other hand. Red bandana, his ponytail flyinggg out back, a 2-foot-long grey beard braided by a Betsy the econoline van drivin' Sheila. Don't be fooled by his toughness, this sweetheart mountain man mystic volunteers twice a year to get folks on wheels some playtime at Cowell's beach by plywood he lays himself. They don't get built like that in California too often, but when they do, they're forged by chainsaws, comedic danger and diesel, so you better sit down, buckle up, and listen.

*Found in a 1987 time capsule. Back when Dale Earnhardt Sr. was President and Ronald Reagan was a Nascar driver, sponsored by Dr. Pepper and Wally World Antiques. Santa Cruz was still a punk rat skater town and surf rock see ya later man. Over the hill, some nerds were making sparkling apple cider and calling it McIntosh.   5/7/25

## Rose

May we remember
the embers and ashes
of the wars of our pasts.
The mothers
who gave their sons
and the fathers
who's brave love
saved everyone.
These gifts of grace
are what frees our days.
Let us honor
each soul we lost
to teach us
to phase
coals to frost.
Now we hold hands
as one
and send
a rose
to the foes
we've crossed.

May the 27th, 2024 | Santa Cruz, CA

# *Saint Augustine*

Friday night alive in San Francisco,
Jerry's b-day and some band
that plays grateful music for the dead.

A reverence for the living with a heckin'
dedication to the joy of being an Earthling!

One day, old folks will smile and wink
about August 1st, 2025.

Until then, may you dance on
into the wind on the moonlight.


8/1/25 | San Francisco, CA
2:55am on a 1971 Remington Streamliner at the Great
Northern.

I dropped this hand typed original poem in the tip
jar of my friend's band, Pfeiffer Beach Hotel
because I had spent all my money to pay rent, buy
gas, and publish this book. Bassist and Fiddler
Wayward Jerry found this artifact in the tip jar
and had a soul synchronicity over the date and
time.
This man carries the musical medicine of Jerry and
we had a bromance moment over our love for the Dead
and the living. Thanks for making my day Jerr <3

## Sainte Vie

Cheap egoic pollution of expensive designer sex
potion lingers in the air after the young man who
plays heroic slithers by. The line is pulsing
with eager anticipation as wafts of vapor float
along, bright eyes dart, and friendly faces meet
once again. Through the LED lights and faint bass
thumps, security ushers the nightlife wildlife
into their lair. ID's checked, earplugs tucked,
and the night begins. Slowly the DJ assembles the
crowd of techno hooligans and rowdy changemakers.
Synthesizers and cymbals pierce the air as low
frequencies wobble against a wooden terrace, no
fakers present. Her glances across the dance
floor signals that she's single, while his eyes
are closed dreaming of the lights in Paris. The
music unites free souls who dance until they're
careless of who's right and wrong, above or
below. After midnight, Sainte Vie rolls into the
rhythm with the tight precision of a conductor
painting the air with tea cups and the elephants
from fantasia. We dance with the grace of a yogi
om shanti om to flow through space like a
ballerina in robes of white satin aglow. Together
we found the beat of our Robot Heart, playfully
advancing the globe's state of art.

2023 | Oakland, CA

# *Sequoian Delight*

Dancing shadows frolic
between aging mushroom networks
of angelic mystery.
The smell of rain
from romantic baby showers
dazzle the noses of playful kin.
Troubled branches
drop aging matter
leaving cover
for a young fern lover.

The cathedral of giants
sees you
just as new parents
look at a child
laughing in defiance.
With pure care,
complete understanding,
and everlasting love so fair.

The shade of ancient trees
hug us as elders
that cast shadows
of shelter
like mother nature's
grand ol' trustees.


10/7/23 | Santa Cruz, CA

## *Shake a leg*

Organic blue jeans have
copper rivets touching denim
as she's dancing to the rhythm.
Hips swaying like a sonorific
vessel that's a glowing ruby
of kinetic beauty.
Thumping drums kick to the guitar's lick.
While her boots imprint their grooves
in the redwood hall warmed by her moves.

8/15/23 | Felton, CA

# Sierran Satori

Dragonflies floating
on Feather River breezes
with zen fountains trickling down stone.
Quartz crystals glimmer in ripples
while the guitar gently wafts
between the willows and the mountains.
We're savoring the friendly banter
on a mosey on Monday
that sends one home to the ocean
where time
began
in waves.

7/8/25 | Quincy, CA


# Slow Motion

Popsicle angels in Subarus
as precious pinecones
BouNce
in that hot July wind.

Rugrats on the bluegrass racetrack,
singing of slow down tortoise town
with stories
about the patience of gemstones in oceans.

It's a surrender to that slowpoke interdepenDance,
turtle toboggan, turn around and try kindness
in slow motion!

7/4/25 | High Sierra Festival in Quincy, CA


It's a High Sierra rendition of West Coast what's
up and where we goin'? Because you and me, we're
born free to see . . . who, how, why we ever wish
to be!

## High Sierra Music Festival & Breathing Under the Sea at 3,400 Feet

I took a melatonin at 12pm on Sunday to let slumberland restore my tired eyes. It had been a waking dream of a 24-hour day submersed in High Sierra Music Festival tomfoolery. I found daytime family vibes and after-hours hooliganism – a ritualistic festivalia. A Saturday night alive if you will. I realized that this type of cultural celebration is more than a party, it's when we remember why we're here and who we are as beings. High Sierra was a precious example of this sacred element of culture that unites us in trying times.

The 33rd annual festival occurred at the Quincy, CA fairgrounds on 4th of July Weekend in 2025. We were 3,455 feet above sea level, surrounded by pine forests as aging oaks shaded the pavement.  The dry air was punctuated with humorous signs on the trees and provoking quotes in comic sans on the porta potties. One such teal sign on a grey honey bucket tinkle tent read: "When I give food to the poor, they call me a saint. When I ask the poor why they have no food, they call me a communist." – Dom Hélder Câmara

Quite the thing to ponder on 4th of July weekend in 2025 at a music festivity. Without pontificating too far out into the weeds, I'll just say that Earth's resources are intended to be communally shared among her beings. See, when the forces of nature conspire for wholesome and equitable creation, we live and long and prosper, so call it a hippie conspiracy theory if you must. Now off my porta potty soap box and back to the fun!

The music I remember from that night was new funk folk with Diggin' Dirt and the bassy brass of Smoked Out Soul. 12 hours earlier, time had dilated into the Kairos clock – the ancient Greek concept for the non-linear experience of sacred time with a mysterious urgency for the present moment's significance. For a more ridiculous understanding of Kairos, it was the 4th of July weekend, and our freak flag was waving in the wind to eclipse the belligerence of the orange man hiding behind the stars and stripes. While we did not check the time or commit petty crimes, we sure did ride some sort of submarine to celebrate the under the sea theme of Saturday's festivities.

To quote Paul McCartney and The Beatles' *Yellow Submarine,* which became a sixties counter-culture anthem sticking its silly thumb at the war machine and their devious contraptions. We sung: "And our friends are all aboard,
Many more of them live next door,
And the band begins to play

We all live in a yellow submarine…".

In the spirit of the artists in the 60's and the hecklers of Saturday Night Live in the 70's, I celebrate the visionary weirdos that sparked our own rock and roll debauchery for good. The kind of freedom that makes our democracy worth fighting over. Thus, I pair those feral revolutionaries with my own curiosity into our Earth. Something like Whole Earth Catalog meets old soul rock and roll. Along that "Muse-Eco" thread, I recently learned that the ocean has been called the lungs of our planet, as phytoplankton generate massive amounts of oxygen while the water provides thermoregulation effects. See now, it wasn't all wild freak power, we were out here conspiring (breathing together) to make sense of this beautiful life.

My fellow sailors included a rockhound and lapidary artist that I'll simply refer to as Peridot. He has traveled the country following rock and roll music, gem fairs, and his spirited heart. Peridot has an east coast Maryland Italian accent with a laidback California coolness, straight up honest and humble. He wears a rainbow tie dye under a well-worn jean jacket with patches from band tours, and a top hat dotted by pins acquired from friends around the country, his dreadlocks now retired leaving behind the wisdom of a balding head. Peridot invited me to this trip to be a poet in the wild and drive up with our 6 foot 4, long black-haired cowboy buddy. The Cowboy would disappear for hours, then return to camp with a grin looking for a cold lager before sauntering off in his dusty boots to find bluegrass tunes or deals on grilled meat. Cowboy is a sweet soul with a toughness about him that says, I'll be there for you bud, just don't touch my hat Mister.

Just before we dove into the depths of the night on the submarine, Peridot and I met up in his RV, then he looked at me mischievously and asked me if I had a tiny screwdriver.

I said: "Dude, why? We need to catch some music, no side quests!" Wanting to avoid the whirlpool of the RV, as I heard live bands playing just a short walk away. He shuffled around in the cabinets, then fished out a set of toy walkie talkies. Laughter ensued and we used a pocket knife to install watch batteries into the gizmos.

The RV was parked on the steep banking of the fairgrounds racetrack, so it felt like we were already at sea in the cabin of a sailboat tugging on an anchor chain. We stumbled around in the dimly lit 1990's Toyota RV, finally getting the walkie talkies to give us a faint transmission. Our 4th buddy, 'Machaca', made his grand entrance. He's a silversmith and jeweler with a smooth velvety voice, whose kind grin and young face made him the sweet hearted hooligan of our crew.

Mr. Machaca peeked around the corner of the RV and declared: "I just wanna do hoodrat shit with my friends!" So Peridot handed him a walkie talkie and a chummy pat on the back.
Machaca walked away then turned back and pressed the talk button to say: "Buzz Lightyear. Do you copy? Buzz Lightyear, time to go deep sea divin' bud."

Machaca and Peridot had a brotherhood that I can only begin to convey, they were playful and vulnerable with each other. Confiding feelings of gratitude after processing existential questions about their creative lives and relationships. But it was time to "do hoodrat shit!"

Around midnight, Peridot packed his mini pit bike, which was an upcycled yellow, red, blue, and green Google campus bike probably found at Shoreline Amphitheater's Dead and Company show with flat tires in a ditch. We rolled out to the late-night music with Peridot flying a black tapestry cape as the moonlight guided us around the now sleepy fairgrounds. He was weaving through the strolling pedestrians on his midnight cruiser machine. Our submarine was merely at the surface, my periscope catching glimpses of Peridot scouting ahead for signs of precious gems of humans swimming in the night.

Machaca had the other walkie talkie, so we identified his 20 outside the music hall talking to a dad named Greg as Ott played electronic music inside. I later learned that Ott's artist alias namesake was Jonathan Ott who just happened to cross the rainbow bridge that weekend. Look both of them up if you want a rabbit hole.

Jelly fish streamed from the ceiling as inflatable shark wearing party people squeezed through the open doors, while Ott did his thing. The only digital music I'd heard all weekend. Greg's 22 month-old son was sound asleep in a wagon, and he told us the story of the family camp activities he had orchestrated for the festival. Something about interactive theater with masks and crafts, super cute family stuff, not hoodrat shit at all. Greg said that his first High Sierra was at 8 years young when he was dropped off with a family friend to roam free. He didn't come back until he was an adult and only then realized the familiar scene, like deja vu, was in fact the very same spot as his childhood adventure.

We shared some nostalgia of summer camp vibes and the full circle magic of being a dad at the same festival. Later that night, I told Machaca that I appreciated his friend Greg. He goes, "Dude, that was my older brother. Love that guy!" and we had a laugh at my moment of obtuseness. The wholesomeness of High Sierra began to sink in, this was a family celebration of what matters: the people we love, the soundtracks of our lives, and a dedication to playful wonder.

The submarine began to dive deeper into the mystery as Peridot and I found ourselves in the after party for Diggin' Dirt and Smoked Out Soul. Our friend Katelyn had given me an after-hours ticket, further instilling a fundamental value of generosity that makes this world go round. We swirled into the early morning current of soulful funk, as we hugged our friends to share moments of gratitude. Katelyn gave us a drink ticket, which I spent on a yerba mate with a healthy tip to her coworkers from the beverage team. Peridot and I embraced as the music really got cooking, smiling at each other realizing the magnitude of the blessings in our lives. Our group of friends danced grinning ear to ear like a school of dolphins surfing wakes in the starlight. Cowboys' usual appearance was notably missing, perhaps he was out of his element with the aquarian energy. I realized that I felt a sense of responsibility for his safety like an older brother. Although I decided that he knew how to swim and had a harmonica to find company. Back to the music, Cowboy would be 'A Okay, partner.'

Smoked Out Soul's brass intensified into a crescendo with the bass synthesizer blasting the low end, with horns harmonizing, as the guitars strung it all together. The sound was alive unlike a streaming algorithm, folks were feeling the energy hum. Kairos. Music. Connection. Real Freedom. We were becoming one. Rainbow lights erupted from the stage with blacklights on the dangling art, the air was humid with a faint smell of craft beer, cannabis, and patchouli. I just smiled and worked my dance groove, unbuttoning my western shirt to let my bare body perspire. Time was now absent as I had no idea of the hour, nor a worry about what was next, this moment was important, who cares why. Kairos and soul music was now at the helm of this submarine that began to feel more like a manta ray gliding through warm tropical waters. My sense of self had left the building and I swam in the harmonic melodies, wandering along the riffs into the vibrancy of the unseen, a corral reef of possibilities in my mind's eye.

Like the end of a dream scene, we spilled out of the venue as a prankster stood at the exit with a flashlight demanding "STAMPS PLEASE, WE NEED TO SEE YOUR STAMPS!" sending the stamp poachers into a panic and the newbies scrambling for an excuse. The gullible ones looked dazed until they saw the small crowd giggling and watching from the side. Cheers and jeers finalized the act of clownery as small groups of friends circled in the crossroads under streetlights. Next was a few hours of poetry writing for me on a dirty couch before sunrise kickball, where my final form of sleep deprived linguistics flowed freely.

On the way to sunrise kickball, I ran into my new friend Sue, an older mother working the booth next to us. We had met earlier that day and just felt a kinship despite the 30 years between our arrivals on Earth. She had just woken up early to get coffee and I was enjoying the birdsongs, so we walked together sharing a wide ranging conversation from relationships, spirituality, to her past life being homeless. I told her about my next book, *A Walk on Earth*, including my story of rediscovering the medicine of a wander in the wild with a journal and the poetry of a morning saunter. I shared the reason I began to walk and write for my soul – exactly 7 years ago this weekend, I was arrested at my first Dead Show after losing myself. I then walked 20 miles home from jail through the blasting fireworks on the 4th of July in a spiritual crisis.

In the years between then and now, I found myself again by simply writing, reading, and walking with love from friends along my meandering journey. She gave me the warmest hug I'd felt in a long time and just looked into my eyes and said, "Thank you and I understand what it's like to be lost. I was homeless for a few years, but I was always ok and you are too." We both felt our eyes well up with the tears of being truly seen by a fellow human. This moment was the lost treasure our submarine ride had been searching for – something so priceless and human: a hug over storytelling between rock and roll generations.

So I bought Sue a cappuccino with the last 7 dollars in my pocket and we shared some more vulnerable stories before wandering toward the berserkers playing kickball. On the way, we found an invisalign tray on the ground and attempted to be the tooth fairies looking for the smile in need of invisible alignment. We left the tray as a hood ornament on a ford van outside the DJ and bid our farewell with one last life changing hug, I moseyed on over to a group of party people to document the kickball madness.

Kickball could be its own short book or film, but I'll leave you with a few prose poetry lines about the morning tradition.

*What began as a friendly game of sandlot style kickball has become ritualistic maverick mayhem. Pure hearted violence at dawn on dewy grass, champagne bottle pulls, and cheap sunglasses with faux fur coats. Sleepless loose cannons lob haymaker kicks at the DJ. Innocent clover counters get mortar-shelled in the outfield by the ruthlessness of a big red ball on the loose. The brass gong shatters our sense of seriousness like the court jester's bells tickling the funny bone. GONG and Bow Down, for the EMPEROR of Embarrassment has arrived to humble your pride!*

This day had begun 24 hours prior in a hot sweat as I emerged from my tent at the top of the hillside campground under Black Oaks and Ponderosa Pines. I awoke to some annoyingly upbeat house music playing at the camp below me. In the distance, I heard finger plucking of an amplified acoustic guitar which matched the mellow noontime sunshine. So I stumbled in a half-cooked stupor toward the guitar. I cured the crankiness of my mid-day wake up with some cherries and walnuts that I found at the bottom of my fanny pack with

a warm meat stick, basically the scavenged break-
fast of an albino crow. Next, I was off to find my
friends and caw at them until they gave me some-
thing shiny like a joke about my liberal use of
sunscreen and dazed look despite the mild weather.
The afternoon sun slowed me down enough to remember
who I was, why I was here, and what matters before
losing myself again to the moonlight music of
summertime in a submarine.

DM

P.S. I later met a couple whose relationship had
blossomed at the festival and so they named their
daughter Sierra. They say "Hi, Sierra" every day.
The father was also the carrier of the red kick
ball for years and this year passed the honor of
delivering the sacred red ball to a man named
Chad who also found love at the festival. Love
finds a way, man.

## *Spring Renew*

On the first day of Spring,
a new brood's virgin song
sings along the stork's wing,
a ballet of shining sun as we all dance along.
At dusk, the first chorus frogs
awake to the bard owl's eerie gong
of a twilight show in the full house of bogs.
Our Monarch's final flutters announce
the finale of black acrobats
before a bobcat winds up to pounce.
What a treat to behold,
an equinox theater
conducted by an accord
with us and our creator.


3/20/24

## *Tattoos and Leather*

Heat waves waft over asphalt
A crow lands on the telephone wire

Traffic looks on with awe, ready to catapult
Rumble pop, gargle, boom boom, black fire

Hell on wheels, bare arms gripping
High handlebars, a stolen riot helmet in velvet
Reminding foolish foes they're tripping.

A young girl passes safely in the crosswalk,
Oblivious to the aging hooligan, the crow goes
squawk!

Traffic cleared, clunk as he shifts into gear,
all clear.
One last puff of the cigar, ding green light.

Off he goes in a roar, wisps of smoke, a spore of
spite,
Drops of oil, and one spun bloke.

5/21/23

## The FADIHA

A slip of the tongue
blushing cheeks, glowing red,
unsung cliches and ringing ears.
Recoiling at the stinging
of a silly dream.
Shooting an arrow again
as if the first one
wasn't sharp enough.
Letting go
of the hot steam
of shame
is easier
than resisting
the urge
to blame
little old me.
A happy accident,
TMI, a freaky mistake,
broccoli in my teeth,
a social belly flop,
a cringe worthy moment.
Admitting the ridiculousness
of saying too much,
laughing at my freakness
like a child
who tooted
in front of his special crush.
I'll be ok,
the blush will fade like **Fadiha**,
returning to play,
and dancing between a parade.

פדיחה or **Fadiha** is a word in Hebrew for an
utterly embarrassing moment that simply describes
this poem. Thank you Renana!

94

## *The Gift of Radical Allowance*

I recognize the feeling of smallness
and fear of making mistakes.
I allow it
unconditionally
and accept life just as it is,
no strings attached.
I inquire with kind curiosity,
totally blind
to what
I've left behind.
Just in time
to learn
that I'm allowed a faux pas,
a crooked tooth, a social blemish,
and I get
to learn
from my errors.
I'm just fine as I am,
perfectly ok
with a scar
or two,
After all,
I'm really no different
than you.

11/15/23 @ Esalen

# *Tidal*

Perched cliffside in a Cypress nest dangling over
the pacific,
I gaze west to where the edge of my mind meets
the horizon.
Reticula sea foam tapestries weave the patterns
of life in patient waves below.
Chipping away at the jagged stubbornness of
sandstone.
A gull swoops in to pluck
a morsel of tidal bounty,
just as I screeched off Highway 1
to this very vista.
The sun breaks through
for just a moment of **satori**
before the late winter earl grey
takes another sip of this coastal day.

# Vows

The silent vow of the poet.

When tragedy arrives early, you cry first because
you've been here before. Do not ask why.

On a normal day, you witness a stranger stop to
chat about life with a lonely soul. No money is
exchanged, just the currency of presence.

When it's sunny, you smile, *Thank you*
and when it rains, you look up to say: "Is there
anything else?"

After doing the dishes, you admire the way water
both remembers and forgets. Your breath slows.

At work in a dull job, you praise your colleagues
for their inherent qualities rather than their
appearance. They laugh it off, but you insist.

If asked what you think about the homelessness
problem, you say: "You mean our community safety
net failure and someone's son or daughter that
misses the way their mom used to hug them?"

On friend's birthdays, you feel called to celebrate
life in general because it's all about who we walk
with and why.

When war breaks out, you cannot sleep without
terror and seek out rituals of grieving for the
casualties lost and the kin of warriors who carry
bloodshed as their ancestry. You write letters in
your mind to the mothers of the soldiers and sing
praise to the helpers who cook, care, and clean up
after the mess of men.

The day you embody your vow as a poet to feel and
know what others simply cannot, is the day that you
will write poetry alive in a kaleidoscope of soul.

Remember that day.  8/20/25 | Santa Cruz, CA

# *We are America.*

Yes, our blue jeans woven in sweatshop India and our obsession
with burning gasoline to drive alone listening to the radio at midnight.
Yes, you too, with the tattoos that I don't understand,
but the story that I love.
Yes, me with my scribbling poetry, promises in my heart,
and nicotine addiction.
Yes. Yes, those of us who worship the man on the cross, desert
prophets, tribal mythology, or the astrology above and below. We are
America.
Yes, you, who goes downtown by broken down car that your auntie
left behind after her opioid overdose last winter. You are America.

Yes, you, who moved here from Mexico to make an honest living,
only to be told to go home by an orange gringo buffoon and his goons.
You are America.
This is your home too and call me if ICE says otherwise.
No, that Fox news hate for folks of color, queer love, the unhoused,
undesirables, liberals, or anybody who asks, "But, why Uncle Sam?"
is not America. That is fear rather than liberty, but we shall overcome.

Yet, those with fear in their hearts and those who receive that hate, they
are both America.
Yes, you, who is afraid and believes the propaganda that started with
Sigmund Freud high on Coca Cola and the war effort rhetoric of his
cousin, Edward Bernays. You are America.
Yes, you who can't pay your taxes because the rent is too high,
your catalytic converter was stolen last month,
and your medicine that was not in the federal budget
after the fighter jets and bombs were bought in bonds by Congress.
And the thief who learned to steal when his mother was working two
jobs, and his father was in prison. We are America.
And the system that quietly quells our rebellious enthusiasm
to create a different way of life, that is not America,
but we shall overcome. We shall overcome.

Yes, the at promise children who learned to read despite education
budget cuts, trauma, and neurodivergence. And the kids whose parents
work hard to keep the lights on, then wait in line at the food bank on

their own dime. They are America. Yes, every child in this land is America.

Yes, you, the artists and lovers, who sprout creations each day like weeds in the cracking sidewalk outside of warehouses with broken windows. And the baristas dreaming of revolution who pour espresso and burn their hands steaming milk before dawn. As they serve people in ties who think that service work is below them until AI closes the last open door on their shocked Pikachu face. You are all America.

Yes, our anxiety about climate change and the plastic in our blood. Yes, your love for the cherry blossoms blooming earlier and earlier at springtime in Washington D.C. and your curiosity about the barrio's music in late summer. You are America.

Yes, the forgotten sounds of the unheard,
the silent graffiti of those without a voice,
and the poems written by those with no other choice
but to live on the streets. Now, THAT is America!

And the lost stories from the first nation's people who tended our land with their bare hands before our settler ancestors killed them. Yes, the slave patrols that became police on payroll and the African souls who sung songs to survive and carry the story of their people. That was America too.

Yes, the tribes who kept their identity secret until a few decades ago and continue to fight to preserve their way of life, land, and language. They were BEFORE America.

Yes, your diary entries and homework from childhood that your mother never read, but saves in a storage unit paid 2 years ahead
as she tucks you into bed each and every night.
Yes, your mother who gave everything she had to raise you right and laughs when you ask for more money. She is America.
Yes, your father who you may never know, but left behind soul homework and your brown eyes. Yes, your father and his dinnertime Rabbi wisdom with his smile knowing you will retell his stories one day. He is America.

Yes, the acts of kindness that we witness each quiet winter, the Mississippi River swelling in spring, the cornfields to West, the cotton fields to the East, and the hands that sow the seeds of family feast and homegrown freedom. We are America.

Remember who America is, was, and will be.
Our wisdom is you and me; it's us.

We Are America and we shall overcome.

We SHALL overcome.

June 25th, 2025 | Santa Cruz, CA

# *We Are One*

I want to imagine a world
where strangers hold hands
to walk each other home.
I want neighbors
to pass apples
through the gaps in their fences.
I want children
to read books to their mom
and sing hallelujah to their grandmother.
I want voters
to write their names
in the concrete of new schools.
I want to see birds chirping

on the telephone wire
that carries the message:
"**We are ONE** and no one will be left behind!"

I want to imagine this world.
I want to make this magic happen for my
children's children.

(**We are One** was hand delivered as part of a
humanitarian mission to Palestine by my friend
Adam in August 2025)

# We've Met

Sip snip, wee potato before a tomato

Snob blob, oh wishful felt, squelch that belch
Ignore the before, forget your fret
Explore the floor, feel the galore, you've met
Tibet

Pretend to befriend, remember the before
There's wisdom in the kingdom, see, hear folklore
Behold the bold, the quintessence of luminescence
Reverence young one,
your gold shines in omnipresence

Afraid of whats not, spooky silly robot
Believe in your curious,
your heart knows the spot

Attend to parts that must contend
Imagine the unexamined, say thanks to the famine

This time, this rhyme, say it again, aloud,
standing proud

2023 | San Francisco, CA

# What It's All About

(originally printed in Shred Magazine)


Riding the rebellion against playing it safe
and cozy
on a crisp dawn like bluebirds in spring.
The surfers of mountain mischief arrive early
after late nights.
They sing the karaoke of stoke
in swashbuckling gondola smoke
and spill stories from past parties
over ice cold keystone lights.
The joy of shared adventure
is the disposition
that flows
through their turns and twists.
They know how to spot something silly
like jean clad skiers
sending it harder
than saucer boy in the movie *Gnar*.
Snowballs down warm backs
and whoops
at pranks
in parking lots.
This is the spirit
of a snowboarder
in a surprise blizzard,
an ethos of radical recreation,
and a glimmer of whimsy
for the city slickers so serious.


2025 | San Luis Obispo, CA

# *Where the Forest Meets the Tides*

(For Santa Cruz, CA)

As the wandering beach bums
wash ashore like driftwood.
The hippies age with grace
though they're still quite misunderstood.
Gossiping locals find solace
when the tourists give them extra space.
Painters, poets, and picturesque
sunsets make for a perfect set
of a drag queen's first bet on bingo burlesque.
Nature nuts and salty wave chasers
Quarrel over the rogue otter
who's just living freely in their home waters.
Strums of the vagabond's guitar
Play the soundtrack to this
bizarre wrinkle
in God's slow burning memoir.

8/14/23

## *You*

You are the whole universe
in a clear vessel of light.
Your ears create music from a flower's bloom.
Your eyes see the moon in the ocean at night.
Your nose smells sage and cedar in an empty room.
Your hands feel
a grandmother's love in a cold stone.
Your toes leave paw prints on moss in the rain.
Your reflection meets God when they are alone.
Your name brings joy to a stranger at home.
Your vessel is now full,
who's cup
will you fill
with a poem
of your own?

January 7th, 2024

# Emotional First Aid

This piece was originally created for a zine preview of my upcoming book, *A Walk on Earth*. May you peacefully walk in beauty, wisdom, and compassion.

Hear is Emotional first aid. Be cool like cucumber lemonade.

1.  Hands on the heart & Say AUM
2.  Breathe! In for 4, Hold for 5, Exhale for 8. Cycle x 3
3.  Extended exhales through pursed lips induces relaxation
4.  Finger on the nose to re-center
5.  Power Pose or Power Walk. Be Brave!
6.  Sing a Tune or Look for the Moon
7.  Hum when you can't sing
8.  CONSENT = May I? + Hearing YES plz
9.  Offer calm breaths as a witness and know when you can/cannot
10. Attune by mirroring emotions and understanding
11. Release the brow, jaw, tongue, neck, hands, feet.
12. Understand and validate, don't fix. Listen and learn.
13. Loops happen until they don't. Allow 'em. Let 'em go.
14. Allow emotional waves to flow without judgment. Yes, and.
15. Practice the sacred pause in conflict.
16. Seek to understand and empathize within their eyes.
17. Accept what you see even if it's not for you. 🖐
18. If you listen long enough, you might learn a thing or three! **<3**

**Nonviolent Tips For Protesting**

Our country will be protesting for the next few years as we suffer the boots of an oppressive regime. We mustn't regress to the fearful tactics of our captives, but rather we shall overcome their violence with our search for limitless compassion and creativity. Reading, speaking out, standing up, and serving the higher good can become our acts of resistance. Clowning, poetry, or dance battles in the face of insanity are also acceptable tactics to disrupt limbic system hijackers.

- Violence can be stopped in its tracks with nonviolence, stillness, and love in silence or in direct action.  Ex: A counter-protestor shouts slurs in your face and shoves you attempting to instigate a fight. YOU: Become a stone, unshakeable like an interdimensional monk. Your hands on your heart, empowered by the chakra palace of jewels.

- War can only end in peace. Fight the battle with peace in mind. Use humor judo and spiritual combat to defend. Be a peaceful warrior clown. You can tell that a war no matter the scale is truly kaput, when everyone grieves in tears and then laughs at the foolishness of violence. Ex: A fight breaks out either verbally or physically. YOU: Become the diplomat and medic. If weapons may be present, do not escalate, and retreat if possible. Stop the skirmish with courageous force like a protective mother bear umpire. If possible, let your paws stretch out and shout at maximum volume: "STOP! Everybody dance now!", then find a salsa partner and start swingin' and steppin'. Attend to anyone who needs care immediately. For more intense battles, you must practice the jiu jitsu bear hug grapple. Hold the combatant as tightly as possible, preventing them from fighting and whisper: "You're safe, I won't hurt you. It's all good, we're just huggin' man."

- Courage is being full of heart - that is the literal etymology of the word. Embody it!

- Unnecessary violence is cowardice and ignorance of the truth, mindful awareness is bravery.

- Remember that the men in uniforms have families and are just as scared as you are. These uniforms are simply a role that they play in society, the badge or baton is not who they are deep inside. They are an imperfect human being who has temporarily been granted power and will have to carry the karma of misusing their status. They are unaware that true courage would be setting down the baton and joining you in protest. Look at them with loving grace, knowing that their soul is inherently divine, yet misguided. Shake them with your wise heart until they remember who they are.

## *Poetry to the People and Our Music*

We passed the typewriter around like a joint of
free expression while Flat Sun Society played
their music to the sunset at the lighthouse and
this what we got:


You can dance it away or sing it in movement.
Eastern wind moody cloud greyface dog bouncing jacks diddles crisp

Breathe, see, wake in the water, dribble, shuffle, in the wake.
Trees defy gravity and they grow against a force unknown.
Zzzbanks roll by and drive your insides insane with curiosity!
roll with the punches for minimal damage. Roll for mood, roll over!

tide             in tide                 winds of change  envelop
us like fog
         rolls              rolls out
the waves crush the mountains of armor around our soul
till we let go and release to its tidal pull
the infinite change drowns our name
from the depths a fire impossible
and we are the flame.


--------

**Pfeiffer Beach Hotel** is the place where you stay
on a full moon of forgiveness because we are only
Earthlings baby and we just do our best to care.

To care for our only home together

as one band,

a band of one in a pile of applause

in a flower field beyond right and left,

the middle of everything

in the presence of freedom.

Heck YES, ok?

10/6/25 | Henry Miller Library in Big Sur, CA

## *Grace*

Saint Francis was here on Saturday to celebrate
our spirit of Earthly unity.

A moon ripening with the fruit of love
in sunshine to see each other
as one Earth walking together.

We're spinning webs of community
to sew our threads
for the magic carpet of the stars.

These times
call for a revolution inside our hearts
to swirl love into cracks
in the armor of warriors.

Our duty is to remember
that every seed is a gift from spirit
and each day is grace for the entire human race.

10/5/25 | Big  Sur, CA

Thank you for reading my truth,
I look forward to hearing yours.

This has been a production of *Imagination Earth*
brought to you by Devin and friends, chai tea,
and that Sequoian Satori. Say hi if you see me
and watch out for my next book, *A Walk On Earth*.

Now, it's up to you. Imagine, Design, and Create
what makes your soul one with the heart of the
world.

www.ingramcontent.com/pod-product-compliance
Lightning Source LLC
Chambersburg PA
CBHW030916140626
46545CB00017B/2372

*  9  7  9  8  2  1  8  7  2  4  7  2  6  *